P9-BZR-190

YOU SHOULD MEET
Roberta Gibb

by Laurie Calkhoven
illustrated by Monique Dong

Ready-to-Read

Simon Spotlight
New York   London   Toronto   Sydney   New Delhi

SIMON SPOTLIGHT
An imprint of Simon & Schuster Children's Publishing Division
1230 Avenue of the Americas, New York, New York 10020
This Simon Spotlight edition March 2018
Text copyright © 2018 by Simon & Schuster, Inc.
Illustrations copyright © 2018 by Monique Dong
All rights reserved, including the right of reproduction in whole or in part in any form.
SIMON SPOTLIGHT, READY-TO-READ, and colophon are registered trademarks
of Simon & Schuster, Inc.
For information about special discounts for bulk purchases, please contact Simon & Schuster Special Sales at
1-866-506-1949 or business@simonandschuster.com.
Manufactured in the United States of America 0218 LAK
2 4 6 8 10 9 7 5 3 1
This book has been cataloged with the Library of Congress.
ISBN 978-1-5344-0972-9 (hc)
ISBN 978-1-5344-0971-2 (pbk)
ISBN 978-1-5344-0973-6 (eBook)

CONTENTS

Introduction

Are there things you love to do? Things that are good for you and make you happy? Like running and feeling the wind in your hair? Or painting a picture? Or conducting a science experiment?

Now imagine that someone told you that you couldn't do the thing you love.

That's what happened to Roberta "Bobbi" Gibb. Bobbi loved to run. Running made her feel free and happy. She ran long distances every day.

Male
participants
ONLY

RULES

When Bobbi wanted to run in the Boston Marathon in 1966, she was told that girls and women were not strong enough to run the 26.2-mile course.

Bobbi knew the men in charge of the race were wrong. So on April 19, 1966, she managed to sneak into the race and became the first woman to finish the Boston Marathon.

No one would give Bobbi Gibb the chance to show what she could do, so she made her *own* chance. And the world of running has never been the same.

If you want to be great at something you love to do, then you should meet Bobbi Gibb. She was the first woman to show the world that women can run far and fast.

Chapter 1
Early Runs

Bobbi Gibb was born on November 2, 1942, in a suburb of Boston, Massachusetts. As a girl, she always loved to run. "I think I started running the minute I could walk," she said. "I just loved to run because somehow it just made me feel more alive."

Bobbi liked to pretend she was a horse galloping through the fields and woods near her Massachusetts home. She ran with her family dogs, and soon neighbors were asking her to run with *their* dogs so their pets would get some exercise too.

In school, Bobbi
played volleyball,
field hockey, and
basketball.

She wasn't allowed to join the cross-country team—running was for boys only. But all through high school, Bobbi kept running through the woods and the fields.

She went to Tufts University in Boston and took classes in sculpture at the Museum of Fine Arts. Her boyfriend was a member of Tufts's cross-country team. He introduced Bobbi to long-distance running. At first it was hard for her, but soon she was running as many as eight miles a day and loving it.

Then one day in 1964, Bobbi heard a family friend talking about the Boston Marathon.

"What's that?" Bobbi asked.

She learned that the Boston Marathon was the oldest long-distance race in the United States.

Since 1897, people have been running the 26.2-mile race from Hopkinton, Massachusetts, into Boston.

It is held every year on Patriots' Day
on the third Monday in April. Patriots'
Day is the anniversary of the Battles of
Lexington and Concord and the beginning
of the American Revolution.

Bobbi didn't believe that anyone could

run as far as 26.2 miles. She went to watch the 1964 race to see if they really could.

Within minutes, Bobbi knew that she wanted to run the race too. At first she didn't realize that there were no women. She only saw a big group of people doing what she loved to do—running.

Chapter 2
Marathon Training

Bobbi watched the marathon for the first time in April 1964. The next day, she started to train for the 1965 race. She had no coach and no plan. She only knew that she wanted to run in the marathon.

No one made running shoes for women back then. Bobbi wore white nurses' shoes and ran every day. Her boyfriend would drive her somewhere on his motorcycle, and Bobbi would run home. She started to run longer and longer distances.

That summer Bobbi and her malamute puppy, Mooty, went on a road trip from Massachusetts all the way across the country to California, just for fun.

As she pulled out of her driveway in her car, she said, "Let's go for a swim, Mooty . . . in the Pacific Ocean."

Mooty wagged her tail and off they went.

Bobbi and Mooty ran for hours every day—in the fields and prairies of the Midwest and the mountains of Colorado and California. It wasn't long before Bobbi could run forty miles at a stretch. She was ready for the Boston Marathon.

Bobbi planned to run in April 1965.

Then she slipped and sprained both of her ankles in March. On Patriots' Day, she watched the race from the sidelines again. As soon as her ankles healed, she started to train again.

That September, Bobbi tested herself by

running in a horse race! She was the only human running in the race. The riders and their horses may have been surprised to find a two-legged runner in the race, but no one tried to stop Bobbi from running. She ran forty miles on the first day. That night she slept in a barn. The next day she ran another twenty-five miles before her knees started to hurt.

By 1966, Bobbi was married and living in San Diego, California. She continued to run on the beach and on mountain trails. One day she set out for a run on the beach at low tide. She didn't notice when she crossed the border into Mexico. By the time she turned around to run back, it was high tide. Bobbi had to run on the road. She had left home without any ID and was stopped at the border between Mexico and the United States. A friend had to come and convince the officials to let her back into the country.

In February 1966, Bobbi wrote to the officials at the Boston Marathon to ask for an application to enter the race. She got a letter back saying that she couldn't run 26.2 miles because she was a woman. The idea of women running long distances made doctors uncomfortable. They didn't know how running a marathon would affect Bobbi. They suggested that she run no more than 1.5 miles at a time.

At first Bobbi was mad. Then she started to laugh. She knew she could run long distances—she had run forty miles at a stretch! She knew that running wasn't bad for her health. She knew she was ready for the marathon, but the marathon wasn't ready for her.

It wasn't long before Bobbi knew that she was going to show the officials how wrong they were.

Chapter 3
The Secret Runner

Bobbi took a four-day bus ride from San Diego to Boston. She arrived on April 18, 1966, the day before the race. She ate a big dinner at her family's home and tried to get some sleep.

Running and jogging suits were not easily available to women back then. So the next morning she put on her black bathing suit and a new pair of boys' sneakers she had bought in California. She was afraid her nurses' shoes would give her away. She pulled on a pair of her brother's shorts and found a navy blue hoodie in the laundry room to hide her ponytail.

Her father wouldn't drive her to the race. He said she was crazy to try to run in a men's race. But Bobbi's mother agreed to take her to Hopkinton. When she got there,

Bobbi jogged around to warm up. Then she hid in the bushes near the start of the race.

At noon, she heard the starter's gun. When about half of the runners had passed her by, Bobbi slipped into the middle of the pack.

It wasn't long before some of the runners saw that she was a woman. There were shouts of, "Hey, there's a girl!"

Bobbi worried about how the men would treat her. But they were happy to have a woman running with them.

Soon, she became hot and took off her sweatshirt. When she did, everyone clearly saw her face and her ponytail and realized she was a woman. "I was afraid I would be arrested," she said.

The men around Bobbi promised her that they wouldn't let anyone stop her from running.

The crowd on the sidelines saw Bobbi and started to cheer. Reporters spotted her and shared the news. The students at Wellesley College, an all-women's school, heard about Bobbi on the radio and rushed to the race to cheer her on.

"I could hear them from a half a mile away," Bobbi said.

The Wellesley students shouted and celebrated as Bobbi ran by.

The cheering crowd kept her going. Then, near the end of the race, she reached what the runners called Heartbreak Hill. Her new boys' sneakers did not fit properly and gave her blisters. Her feet felt like they were on fire.

Bobbi was barely moving. Would she be able to finish the race?

ESLEY

girl Power!

W

Chapter 4
Victory!

Bobbi kept putting one tired foot in front
of the other. Her blisters made her feel like
she was running on tacks. But Bobbi knew
she couldn't give up or the men in charge
of the race would say that they had been
right all along. Now she just wanted to
make it through the last three miles. She
couldn't wait to cross the finish line and
drink some water.

The winners of the race had finished
an hour before. Bobbi thought she would
cross the finish line and quietly go home.
But that's not what happened.

Newspapers were waiting to snap a picture of the first woman to run the marathon. Thousands of people had turned out to watch the marathon, especially to see Bobbi. Even the governor of Massachusetts, John Volpe, was waiting to shake her hand.

FINISH

She came in as number 126 of 540 runners. Bobbi had finished the race ahead of three-fourths of the male runners.

After talking to the press, Bobbi followed the other runners to a cafeteria where the participants were eating. Two guards wouldn't let Bobbi in.

"Men only," they told her.

Bobbi just laughed. She had finished her race. She had proved that women could run marathons. No one could tell her ever again that women couldn't run!

Boston Blonde 1st Girl
to Run Marathon

Record   American

Boston Bride First
Gal to Ru
Marath

Girl!

The next day, Bobbi's picture was on the front page of newspapers across the country and around the world. Her story was on the radio and on the television news. No one could believe that a woman had finished the Boston Marathon, especially because she was faster than many of the men. Even so, most of the news stories referred to Bobbi as a bride or a married woman instead of as a runner. Some didn't even print her name!

Bobbi didn't let that bother her. Instead she wondered what else girls and women could do that society told them they couldn't. She hoped her victory would encourage other women to break more barriers.

Chapter 5
Never Give Up

Even though the Boston Athletic Association still didn't let women into the race, the next year Bobbi ran again. Race officials linked arms at the finish line and wouldn't let Bobbi cross. But she didn't give up. She came back to Boston again in 1968 and ran the race a third time. Other women ran with her in those races. But it wasn't until 1972 that the Boston Athletic Association changed its rules. Finally, women could officially enter the Boston Marathon.

Bobbi went on to do many other things in her life. She became a mother, a lawyer, and an artist. She created paintings and sculptures. But she never stopped running.

In 1984, Bobbi was asked to sculpt three trophies for the top three female marathoners at the US Olympic trials. These top three runners would go on to race for the United States in the 1984 Olympics in California. This was the first time there would be a women's marathon held at the Olympics. American Joan Benoit Samuelson won one of those trophies and went on to win the gold medal in the women's marathon at the 1984 Olympic Games.

In 1996, at the one hundredth running of the Boston Marathon, the Boston Athletic Association finally recognized Bobbi's accomplishments. She was given a medal. Her name was finally added to the Boston Marathon Memorial.

Bobbi still loves to run and does so every day.

She showed the world that girls are strong enough to do anything boys can do. Now that you've met her, don't you agree?

BUT WAIT...

THERE'S MORE!

Turn the page to learn more about female runners, the history of the marathon, and how to stay healthy so you can race too.

Be Strong Like Bobbi!

Here are tips for growing up strong and healthy.

Drink up.

Your body is about 70 percent water. You should drink eight glasses of water a day—more if you're being active and exercising.

If you feel sick to your stomach or dizzy after exercising, you might be dehydrated (say: dee-HI-drayt-ed). That means you don't have enough water in your body. Tell a grown-up right away.

Warm up.

This means to get your muscles moving a little bit before working them really hard. Warming up helps prevent injuries like pulled muscles.

For example, if you're going to be running, jog for three minutes first.

Be active.

Try to get your body moving sixty minutes a day, five days a week. You don't have to do it all at once. You can get active for thirty minutes twice a day or fifteen minutes four times a day. As long as it adds up to sixty minutes! Make it fun. Race with your friends. Play basketball, soccer, or tag! Or put on your favorite song and dance. Get your heart pumping and your body moving.

Stretch out.

Gently stretching your muscles helps prevent injuries. Make sure to stretch after your muscles have been warmed up, like after walking, playing, or exercising.

Eat!

Eat breakfast, lunch, and dinner each day. If you are not able to eat three meals each day, talk to a trusted adult, like a parent, teacher, or school nurse. Ask about breakfast and lunch programs at your school and library. There are other resources available too!

Learn about the food groups. Healthy grains, fruits, vegetables, proteins, and dairy give you energy so you can grow strong. Sugar and salt slow you down.

Make healthy choices.

- Drink water instead of sugary drinks.
- Choose fresh fruits and vegetables over salty, sugary snacks.
- Try to eat the rainbow! Fruits and vegetables come in all colors: red, orange, yellow, green, blue, and purple. Try to eat three different colors of fruits or vegetables a day.
- Pick whole wheat bread instead of white when you can.

Sleep!

If you are between five and ten years old, you need ten hours of sleep or more per day!

Unstoppable Change

A year after Roberta Gibb first ran the Boston Marathon, another female runner made headlines around the world.

Kathrine Switzer was a college runner with marathon dreams. She knew women were not allowed to run in long-distance races, but she registered for the Boston Marathon anyway. She signed her name "K. V. Switzer" on the entry form. The race officials assumed she was a man and sent her a race bib. Her number was 261.

About four miles into the marathon, a race official saw that Kathrine was a woman and therefore not allowed to participate. He ran after her and tried to stop her. He grabbed her sweatshirt and said, "Give me those numbers!" He wanted her to remove her race bib. Kathrine's coach and another runner held back the official. Kathrine kept running. She completed the Boston Marathon as the first registered female runner.

By evening, photographs of Kathrine's struggle were published in newspapers around the world. "I knew I was going to spend much of my life both proving that women deserve opportunities to run, and creating them," she said.

Kathrine continued to push for women to be allowed into the Boston Marathon and finally succeeded in 1972. She created the Avon International Running Circuit in 1978 so women would have more places to run. She went on to push for the women's marathon to be an Olympic sport. She succeeded in 1984.

In 2017, Kathrine ran the Boston Marathon again to commemorate the fiftieth anniversary of her historic run. It was her fortieth marathon. She continues to inspire women to push themselves to achieve their dreams.

Did You Know . . . ?

• The marathon was named after the city of Marathon, Greece. The long-distance running race got its start from a legend in which Pheidippides, a runner in the Greek army, ran from Marathon to Athens to deliver a message that the Greek army had just won an important battle against the Persian army. He ran approximately twenty-six miles.

• Why is a marathon 26.2 miles long? 26.2 is a strange number. Why not twenty-five miles or twenty-six miles? The marathon became exactly 26.2 miles long in 1908 when the Olympic games were held in London, England. Queen Alexandra asked that the race start on the Windsor Castle lawn so that the children in the nursery could watch from their window. She also requested that the race end in front of the royal box. That route, which measured 26.2 miles, stuck. In 1921, the official standard for a marathon was set at 26.2 miles, and that is still the standard today.

• The record for most marathons run on consecutive days is 365! Belgian runner Stefaan Engels, knows as the

"Marathon Man," set the record in 2011, at age forty-nine!

• The oldest person to complete a marathon was one hundred years old at the time. He was an Indian man named Fauja Singh. And guess what? Fauja didn't even start running until he was eighty-nine years of age. It's never too late!

• Twelve of the world's top twenty distance runners of all time are members of the Kalenjin tribe of northwest Kenya.

• In a recent study, when asked what food they couldn't live without, most runners named bananas as their most adored foodie fix! The potassium and magnesium in bananas may help protect runners from muscle cramps, so it's no wonder bananas are their favorite snack!

Now that you've met Bobbi, what have you learned?

1. According to Bobbi, when did she start running?

a. as soon as she could walk   b. in high school   c. in college

2. Which is the oldest marathon in the United States?

a. New York Marathon   b. Los Angeles Marathon   c. Boston Marathon

3. What did Bobbi wear when training for her first marathon?

a. sneakers   b. nurses' shoes   c. boots

4. What kept Bobbi from running in the 1965 Boston Marathon?

a. sprained ankles   b. bad weather   c. fear

5. Bobbi was rejected from the 1966 Boston Marathon because she was what?

a. a woman   b. too young   c. not fast enough

6. What did the people watching the 1966 Boston Marathon do when they saw that Bobbi was a woman?

a. booed   b. protested   c. cheered

7. Bobbi finished the race ahead of how many of the other runners?

a. none   b. most   c. all

8. Bobbi went on to become a mother, artist, and what else?

a. fencer   b. teacher   c. lawyer

9. When did Bobbi receive a medal for running in the Boston Marathon?

a. 1996   b. 2016   c. 1976

10. Bobbi showed the world that women are strong enough to do what?

a. run 1.5 miles   b. wear sneakers   c. run marathons

Answers: 1.a 2.c 3.b 4.a 5.a 6.c 7.b 8.c 9.a 10.c

REPRODUCIBLE